Get pupils' knowledge in order with CGP!

Looking for a simple way to help pupils learn all the key facts and methods for Year 5 Maths? Well, look no further — this Knowledge Organiser is the perfect solution!

We've condensed each topic down to the essentials, so it covers exactly what pupils need, with clear diagrams and tables.

And that's not all! There's a matching Year 5 Maths Knowledge Retriever — a great way of making sure pupils have got to grips with the content of every page.

CGP – still the best! ☺

Our sole aim here at CGP is to produce the highest quality books — carefully written, immaculately presented and dangerously close to being funny.

Then we work our socks off to get them out to you — at the cheapest possible prices.

Published by CGP

Editors: Sarah George, Ruth Greenhalgh, Rachel Hickman, Sean McParland, Ali Palin,
Sarah Pattison and Dave Ryan.

With thanks to Alison Griffin and Glenn Rogers for the proofreading.

With thanks to Jan Greenway for the copyright research.

ISBN: 978 1 78908 869 4

Printed by Elanders Ltd, Newcastle upon Tyne.
Clipart from Corel®

Based on the classic CGP style created by Richard Parsons.

Contents

Number Basics

Place Value

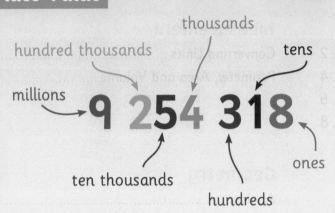

thousands

hundred thousands

tens

millions

9 254 318

ten thousands

hundreds

ones

This number is:

nine million, two hundred and fifty-four thousand, three hundred and eighteen.

Comparing and Ordering

To compare two or more numbers, look at the digits in each place value column.

> means "is greater than".

< means "is less than".

Ascending order: numbers go from smallest to biggest.

Descending order: numbers go from biggest to smallest.

Partitioning

You can partition numbers using **place value**.

The number **3 487 502** can be partitioned into 3 millions, 4 hundred thousands, 8 ten thousands, 7 thousands, 5 hundreds and 2 ones.

M	HTh	TTh	Th	H	T	O
3	4	8	7	5	0	2

There aren't any tens.

3 487 502 = 3 000 000 + 400 000 + 80 000 + 7000 + 500 + 2

Numbers can be partitioned in other ways too:

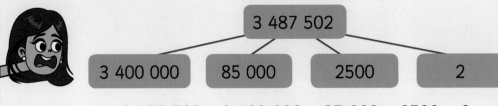

3 487 502 = 3 400 000 + 85 000 + 2500 + 2

Negative numbers are numbers less than zero.

Use number lines to calculate with them.

To find the difference between two numbers, count the places between them.

EXAMPLE

Find the difference between 5 and –3.

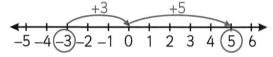

Between –3 and 0 there are 3 places.

Between 0 and 5 there are 5 places.

So the difference is 3 + 5 = 8.

EXAMPLE

Use < or > to make the statement below correct.

325 604 __ 305 624

Both numbers have 3 hundred thousands.

325 604   305 624

2 is greater than 0.

So 325 604 > 305 624

To add, find your starting point and count on. To subtract, find your starting point and count back.

EXAMPLE

What is –1 – 12?

1 Start at –1.

2 Count back 10 places.

3 Then count back 2 places.

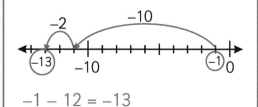

–1 – 12 = –13

EXAMPLE

Put these numbers into ascending order:

132, 1051, 211, 141

1051 is the only number with a thousands digit, so it's the biggest.

211 has 2 hundreds, 132 and 141 have 1 hundred. 2 is bigger than 1, so 211 is next biggest.

141 has 4 tens, 132 has 3 tens. 4 is bigger than 3, so 141 is bigger.

So the order is 132, 141, 211, 1051.

Powers of 10 and Rounding

Counting in Powers of 10

Power of 10: a 1 followed by zeros. E.g. 10, 100, 1000, 10 000, etc.

To count on in steps of a power of 10, add 1 to the digit matching the power.

To count on from **25 384** in steps of **100**, add 1 to the hundreds digit each time.

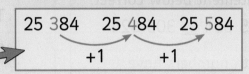

25 384   25 484   25 584
          +1   +1

To count on in steps of **10 000**, add 1 to the ten thousands digit each time.

To count back in steps of a power of 10, subtract 1 from the digit matching the power.

EXAMPLE

Count back from 18 324 in steps of 1000. Stop after 3 steps.

18 324   17 324   16 324   15 324
     −1   −1   −1

Multiplying by 10, 100, 1000

To multiply by **10**, move all the digits **1** place to the left.

$$51 \times 10 = 510$$

To multiply by **100**, move all the digits **2** places to the left.

$$51 \times 100 = 5100$$

To multiply by **1000**, move all the digits **3** places to the left.

$$51 \times 1000 = 51\ 000$$

Dividing by 10, 100, 1000

To divide by **10**, move all the digits **1** place to the right.

$$350 \div 10 = 35$$

To divide by **100**, move all the digits **2** places to the right.

$$350 \div 100 = 3.5$$

To divide by **1000**, move all the digits **3** places to the right.

$$350 \div 1000 = 0.35$$

Rounding Whole Numbers

You can round whole numbers to the nearest 10, 100, 1000, etc.

1 Find the two possible answers.

2 Look at the digit to the right of the place being rounded to — the **decider**.

3 If the decider is less than 5, then round down. If the decider is 5 or more, then round up.

EXAMPLE

Round 2067 to the nearest ten.

2067 is between 2060 and 2070.

The decider is 7 $\longrightarrow$ 2067

7 is more than 5,

so round up to 2070.

$$32.8 \times 1000 = 32\,800$$

Move all the digits **3** places to the left.

TTh	Th	H	T	O		tth
			3	2	.	8
3	2	8	0	0	.	

Don't add a zero here.

Fill spaces before the decimal point with zeros.

The number of zeros tells you how many places to move the digits.

$$6.3 \div 100 = 0.063$$

O		tth	hth	thth
6	.	3		
0	.	0	6	3

Move all the digits 2 places to the right.

Fill the space between the decimal point and the first digit with zeros.

Fill space before the decimal point with a zero.

Number Facts

Multiples

Multiples of a number: the numbers in its times table. E.g. the multiples of 7 are 7, 14, 21, 28, etc.

Rules for spotting multiples:

Multiples of 2	End in even numbers or 0
Multiples of 5	End in 5 or 0
Multiples of 10	End in 0

Common multiple of two numbers: a number that is a multiple of both numbers.

> **EXAMPLE**
>
> Find a common multiple of 8 and 12.
>
> First few multiples of 8:
> 8   16   (24)   32
>
> First few multiples of 12:
> 12   (24)   36   48
>
> 24 is a common multiple of 8 and 12.

Factors

Factors of a number: whole numbers that divide exactly into it.

Factors come in pairs that multiply together to give the number.

If there's an odd number of factors, the middle factor multiplies by itself.

Square and Cube Numbers

Square number: the number you get when you multiply a number by itself.

$4 \times 4 = 4$ squared $= 4^2 = 16$

$6 \times 6 = 6$ squared $= 6^2 = 36$

$9 \times 9 = 9$ squared $= 9^2 = 81$

Square numbers are the areas in this pattern of squares.

$1 \times 1 = 1$
$2 \times 2 = 4$
$3 \times 3 = 9$

The first few square numbers are 1, 4, 9, 16 and 25.

EXAMPLE

Find all the factor pairs of 12.

12   1 × 12   2 × 6   3 × 4

The factor pairs are 1 and 12, 2 and 6, and 3 and 4.

Common factor of two numbers: a number that is a factor of both numbers.

EXAMPLE

What are the common factors of 15 and 27?

Factors of 15: (1) (3) 5   15

Factors of 27: (1) (3) 9   27

1 and 3 are the common factors of 15 and 27.

Roman Numerals

Roman numerals are letters that represent numbers.

I = 1	V = 5	X = 10	L = 50
C = 100	D = 500	M = 1000	

1 Add together numerals that are the same. ⟶ III = 3

2 Smaller numeral before a bigger one — subtract. ⟶ IX = 9

3 Smaller numeral after a bigger one — add. ⟶ MC = 1100

4 Convert numbers in stages:

$$\underline{LXXIX}$$

50 + 10 + 10 = 70   10 – 1 = 9

70 + 9 = 79

Cube number: the number you get when you multiply a number by itself twice.

2 × 2 × 2 = 2 cubed = 2^3 = 8

4 × 4 × 4 = 4 cubed = 4^3 = 64

5 × 5 × 5 = 5 cubed = 5^3 = 125

The first few cube numbers are 1, 8, 27 and 64.

 1 × 1 × 1 = **1**

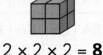 2 × 2 × 2 = **8**

 3 × 3 × 3 = **27**

Cube numbers are the volumes in this pattern of cubes. ⟶

Prime Numbers

Prime Numbers

Prime number: has exactly two factors — 1 and itself.

A number with more than two factors is called a composite number.

1 **1** is not a prime number — it only has 1 factor.

2 All prime numbers end in 1, 3, 7 or 9, except for 2 and 5.

3 **2** is the only even prime number.

The prime numbers below 20 are:

2, 3, 5, 7, 11, 13, 17 and 19.

Prime Factors

Whole numbers that aren't prime (apart from 1) are made up of prime numbers multiplied together.

These numbers are called **prime factors**.

The shaded squares show the prime numbers up to 100.

1	2	3	4	5	6	7	8	9	10
11	12	13	14	15	16	17	18	19	20
21	22	23	24	25	26	27	28	29	30
31	32	33	34	35	36	37	38	39	40
41	42	43	44	45	46	47	48	49	50
51	52	53	54	55	56	57	58	59	60
61	62	63	64	65	66	67	68	69	70
71	72	73	74	75	76	77	78	79	80
81	82	83	84	85	86	87	88	89	90
91	92	93	94	95	96	97	98	99	100

To find prime factors:

1 Write down any factor pair of the number.

2 Split composite numbers into factor pairs.

3 Repeat until all the factors are prime.

Checking if a Number is Prime

1 Does the number end in 1, 3, 7 or 9?

Yes → **2** Does it have exactly two factors?

Yes → **3** Prime

No → Not prime

No → Is the number 2 or 5?

Yes → Prime

No → Not prime

EXAMPLE

Which prime numbers multiply together to make 63?

7 is a prime number.

Split 9 into a factor pair.

63
/ \
7   9
   / \
  3   3

63 = 7 × 3 × 3, so the prime numbers are 3, 3 and 7.

EXAMPLE

Which of the following numbers are prime numbers?

27   53   49   62   75   31

27, 53, 49, and 31 end in a 1, 3, 7 or 9, so could be prime.

Factors of 27: 1, 3, 9 and 27

Factors of 53: 1 and 53

Factors of 49: 1, 7 and 49

Factors of 31: 1 and 31

So 53 and 31 are prime numbers.

EXAMPLE

Find the prime factors of 24.

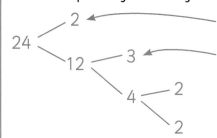

24
/ \
2   12
    / \
   3   4
      / \
     2   2

2 is a prime number. Split 12 into a factor pair.

3 is a prime number. Split 4 into a factor pair.

All of the factors are prime numbers, so the prime factors of 24 are 2 and 3.

Adding and Subtracting

Adding in Columns

Work out 62 832 + 13 795.

1 Add the **ones** column.

```
  TTh Th  H  T  O
   6  2  8  3  2
+  1  3  7  9  5
_____
               7
```

2 Add the **tens** column.

```
  TTh Th  H  T  O
   6  2  8  3  2
+  1  3  7  9  5
_____
            2  7
         1
```

3 + 9 = 12, so put 2 in the **tens** column and carry **1** to the **hundreds** column.

3 Add the **hundreds** column.

```
  TTh Th  H  T  O
   6  2  8  3  2
+  1  3  7  9  5
_____
         6  2  7
      1  1
```

Remember to add any carried digits.

8 + 7 + 1 = 16, so put **6** in the **hundreds** column and carry 1 to the thousands column.

Subtracting in Columns

Find 835.3 – 516.2

1 Line up the decimal points.

```
  H  T  O . t
  8  3  5 . 3
– 5  1  6 . 2
_____
          . 1
```

2 Subtract the tenths: 3 – 2 = 1.

3 Subtract the ones. You can't do 5 – 6, so exchange 1 ten for 10 ones. Then 15 – 6 = 9.

```
  H  T  O . t
     2  1
  8  3  5 . 3
– 5  1  6 . 2
_____
        9 . 1
```

4 Subtract the tens: 2 – 1 = 1
Then the hundreds: 8 – 5 = 3

```
  H  T  O . t
     2  1
  8  3  5 . 3
– 5  1  6 . 2
_____
  3  1  9 . 1
```

So 835.3 – 516.2 = 319.1

Addition and Subtraction Problems

Read the question and pick out the key information.

Then turn it into number sentences.

EXAMPLE

Max has £7.50. He is given £5.95, then he spends £10.40. How much money does he have now?

Max had £7.50 + £5.95 = £13.45

Now Max has £13.45 − £10.40 = £3.05

---

 4 Add the thousands column and then the **ten thousands** column.

TTh	Th	H	T	O
6	2	8	3	2
+ 1	3	7	9	5
7 6	6	6	2	7
	1	1		

So 62 832 + 13 795 = 76 627

Mental Calculations

EXAMPLE

Use partitioning to find 5024 + 3090.

$$5024 + 3090$$

$$5000 + 3000 + 20 + 90 + 4$$

$$8000 + 110 + 4 = 8114$$

For decimal sums, do a whole-number calculation and then adjust the answer.

EXAMPLE

What is 9.3 − 4.8?

Multiply both numbers by 10 to get whole numbers:

$$93 - 48 = 45$$

Adjust by dividing by 10:

$$9.3 - 4.8 = 45 \div 10 = 4.5$$

Checking Answers

You can use rounding to estimate answers.

EXAMPLE

Li works out that 38.9 − 17.3 = 31.6. Use estimation to check Li's answer.

To the nearest whole number, 38.9 rounds to 39 and 17.3 rounds to 17.

$$39 - 17 = 22$$

This is not close to 31.6, so Li is wrong.

Multiplying and Dividing

Long Multiplication

Partition the 2-digit number.
Multiply by each part separately.
Then add together.

EXAMPLE

Calculate 2317 × 23.

1 Find 2317 × 3.

```
    2 3 1 7
×       2 3
    6 9 5 1
          2
```

3 × 7 = 21, so put
the 1 in the ones column
and carry 2 to the tens column.

3 × 10 = 30, plus the carried 20 is 50.

2 Find 2317 × 20.

```
    2 3 1 7
×       2 3
    6 9 5 1
  4 6 3 4 0
        1
```

20 × 10 = 200,
plus the carried
100 is 300.

20 × 7 = 140, so put 4 and 0
in the correct columns and
carry 1 to the hundreds column.

Written Division

EXAMPLE

What is 4682 divided by 5?

1
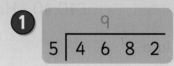
```
        9
5 | 4 6 8 2
```

5 × 9 = 45, so 5 goes into 46
nine times with 1 left over.

3 Add the answers together.

```
      2 3 1 7
×         2 3
      6 9 5 1    ← 1
+   4 6 3 4 0    ← 2
    5 3 2 9 1
    1 1
```

2317 × 23 = 6951 + 46 340
= 53 291

Wordy Problems

Pick out the key information
and write the problem as
a number sentence.

②

$$\begin{array}{r} 9\ 3 \\ 5\overline{)4\ 6\ ^18\ ^32} \end{array}$$

$5 \times 3 = 15$, so 5 goes into 18
three times with 3 left over.

③

$$\begin{array}{r} 9\ 3\ 6\ \text{r}\ 2 \\ 5\overline{)4\ 6\ ^18\ ^32} \end{array}$$

$5 \times 6 = 30$, so 5 goes into 32
six times with 2 left over.

So $4682 \div 5 = 936$ remainder 2

The remainder can be
written as a fraction ⟶ $936\frac{2}{5}$

or as a decimal. ⟶ 936.4

Mental Calculations

To multiply in your head,
change the calculation to
something easier to deal with.

EXAMPLE

Tony swims 28 lengths every day.
How many lengths does he swim
in 6 days?

Tony swims 28×6 lengths in total.

$28 = 30 - 2$, so work out

30×6 and 2×6, then subtract:

$30 \times 6 = 180$ and $2 \times 6 = 12$

He swims $180 - 12 = 168$ lengths.

You can use partitioning to divide.

EXAMPLE

Use partitioning to find $114 \div 6$.

$114 = 60 + 54$

So work out $60 \div 6$ and $54 \div 6$,

then add the answers together:

$60 \div 6 = 10$ and $54 \div 6 = 9$.

So $114 \div 6 = 10 + 9 = 19$.

EXAMPLE

Rhea spent £8. Anil spent three times as much money as Rhea.
Cleo spent one quarter of what Anil spent. How much money did Cleo spend?

Anil spent £8 × 3 = £24. So Cleo spent £24 ÷ 4 = £6.

Fractions

Equivalent Fractions

Equivalent fractions look different, but are equal.

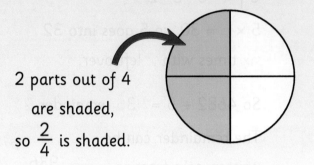
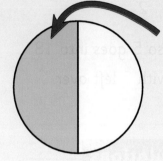

2 parts out of 4 are shaded, so $\frac{2}{4}$ is shaded.

1 part out of 2 is shaded, so $\frac{1}{2}$ is shaded.

The same amount of each circle is shaded, so $\frac{2}{4}$ is equivalent to $\frac{1}{2}$.

Improper Fractions and Mixed Numbers

improper fraction	a fraction where the numerator is bigger than the denominator
mixed number	has a whole number part and a fraction part

> Fractions where the numerator is smaller than the denominator are called "proper fractions".

You can change between improper fractions and mixed numbers:

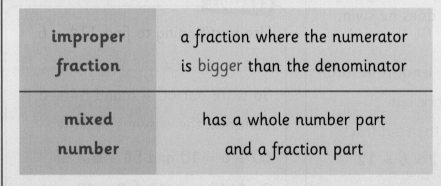

$\frac{12}{7}$ is the same as $1\frac{5}{7}$

12 sevenths

1 whole and

12 − 7 = 5 sevenths

$2\frac{3}{8}$ is the same as $\frac{19}{8}$

2 wholes = 16 eighths.

Plus 3 eighths

19 eighths

To find equivalent fractions, multiply or divide the numerator and denominator by the same number.

$$\overset{\times 5}{\underset{\times 5}{\frac{2}{3} \rightarrow \frac{10}{15}}} \qquad \overset{\div 4}{\underset{\div 4}{\frac{16}{20} \rightarrow \frac{4}{5}}}$$

1 tenth is equivalent to 10 hundredths.

$$\overset{\times 10}{\underset{\times 10}{\frac{7}{10} \rightarrow \frac{70}{100}}}$$

Ordering Fractions

If the fractions have the same denominator, compare the numerators. Fractions with bigger numerators are bigger.

For fractions with different denominators:

1 Find a common denominator.

2 Write all the fractions as equivalent fractions using the common denominator.

3 Compare the numerators.

EXAMPLE

Write $\frac{3}{8}$, $\frac{1}{4}$ and $\frac{5}{12}$ in order from smallest to largest.

1 24 is a common multiple of 8, 4 and 12, so make this the denominator.

2
$$\overset{\times 3}{\underset{\times 3}{\frac{3}{8} \rightarrow \frac{9}{24}}} \qquad \overset{\times 6}{\underset{\times 6}{\frac{1}{4} \rightarrow \frac{6}{24}}} \qquad \overset{\times 2}{\underset{\times 2}{\frac{5}{12} \rightarrow \frac{10}{24}}}$$

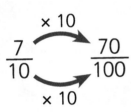
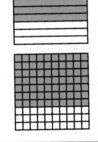

3 From smallest to largest, the order is $\frac{6}{24}$, $\frac{9}{24}$, $\frac{10}{24}$.

Change the fractions back to the ones in the question: $\frac{1}{4}$, $\frac{3}{8}$, $\frac{5}{12}$

Fraction Calculations

Adding and Subtracting — Same Denominator

When fractions have the same denominator, add or subtract the numerators.

EXAMPLE

What is $\frac{5}{11} + \frac{8}{11}$?

Add the numerators:

$$\frac{5}{11} + \frac{8}{11} = \frac{5+8}{11} = \frac{13}{11}$$

You can also write this as $1\frac{2}{11}$.

EXAMPLE

What is $\frac{18}{13} - \frac{9}{13} + \frac{3}{13}$?

Add and subtract the numerators:

$$\frac{18}{13} - \frac{9}{13} + \frac{3}{13} = \frac{18-9+3}{13}$$

$$= \frac{12}{13}$$

Adding and Subtracting — Different Denominators

You can only add or subtract fractions if they have the same denominator.

If the denominators are different:

Find equivalent fractions that have a common denominator.

↓

Add or subtract the numerators.

EXAMPLE

What is $\frac{5}{6} + \frac{4}{9}$?

18 is a common multiple of 6 and 9, so make 18 the denominator.

$$\frac{5}{6} \xrightarrow{\times 3} \frac{15}{18} \qquad \frac{4}{9} \xrightarrow{\times 2} \frac{8}{18}$$
$$\times 3 \qquad \qquad \times 2$$

$$\frac{5}{6} + \frac{4}{9} = \frac{15}{18} + \frac{8}{18} = \frac{15+8}{18} = \frac{23}{18}$$

Multiplying Fractions

To multiply a whole number by a fraction, divide by the denominator and multiply by the numerator.

Or you can multiply first, then divide, if that's easier.

When you're dealing with fractions, "of" means "times".

EXAMPLE

What is $\frac{2}{9}$ of 36?

Divide by the denominator:

$36 \div 9 = 4$

Multiply by the numerator:

$4 \times 2 = 8$

So $\frac{2}{9}$ of 36 = 8

Change mixed numbers to improper fractions before adding or subtracting them.

EXAMPLE

What is $1\frac{3}{10} - \frac{8}{15}$?

$1\frac{3}{10} = \frac{10}{10} + \frac{3}{10} = \frac{13}{10}$

30 is a common multiple of 10 and 15, so use 30 as the common denominator.

$$\overset{\times 3}{\underset{\times 3}{\frac{13}{10} \rightleftarrows \frac{39}{30}}} \qquad \overset{\times 2}{\underset{\times 2}{\frac{8}{15} \rightleftarrows \frac{16}{30}}}$$

$1\frac{3}{10} - \frac{8}{15} = \frac{39}{30} - \frac{16}{30} = \frac{23}{30}$

Partition mixed numbers into whole numbers and fractions, then multiply each part separately.

EXAMPLE

Work out $2\frac{3}{4} \times 8$.

$2\frac{3}{4} = 2 + \frac{3}{4}$

Work out 2×8: $2 \times 8 = 16$

$\frac{1}{4} \times 8 = 8 \div 4 = 2$,

so $\frac{3}{4} \times 8 = 2 \times 3 = 6$.

So $2\frac{3}{4} \times 8 = 16 + 6 = 22$

You could also change mixed numbers into improper fractions instead, if that's easier.

Decimals

Tenths, Hundredths and Thousandths

Decimals are a way to write a number that isn't a whole number.

The first few places after the decimal point are the tenths, hundredths and thousandths.

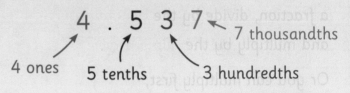

4 . 5 3 7

4 ones   5 tenths   3 hundredths   7 thousandths

$0.1 = \text{one tenth} = \dfrac{1}{10}$

$0.01 = \text{one hundredth} = \dfrac{1}{100}$

$0.001 = \text{one thousandth} = \dfrac{1}{1000}$

1 tenth = 100 thousandths

1 hundredth = 10 thousandths

EXAMPLE

Write 0.103 as a fraction.

This has 103 thousandths.

So the fraction is $\dfrac{103}{1000}$.

Rounding Decimals

0.819   3rd d.p.

1st d.p.   2nd d.p.

Each number after the decimal point is called a decimal place (d.p.).

To round decimals:

1 Count the number of decimal places you need to keep.

2 Look at the next digit to the right — the **decider**.

3 If the decider is less than 5, round down. If the decider is 5 or more, round up.

EXAMPLE

Round 4.57 to 1 decimal place.

4.5|7

You need to keep 1 decimal place, so the decider is the hundredths digit.

7 is bigger than 5, so round up to 4.6

Writing Decimals as Fractions

To write a decimal as a fraction, look at the tenths, hundredths or thousandths.

$$0.7 = 7 \text{ tenths} = \frac{7}{10}$$

$$0.19 = 19 \text{ hundredths} = \frac{19}{100}$$

EXAMPLE

Write 2.081 as a fraction.

This has 2 ones and 81 thousandths.

You can write this as a mixed number: $2\frac{81}{1000}$

Ordering Decimals

To put decimals in order, look at the digits in each place value column.

If the digits in one column are the same, compare the digits in the next column.

EXAMPLE

Put these decimals in order from smallest to largest: 0.579, 1.34, 0.6, 0.572

Write the numbers in place value columns, keeping the decimal points in line.

0.579	0.579	0.579	0.572
1.340	0.600	0.572	0.579
0.600	0.572	0.600	0.600
0.572	1.340	1.340	1.340

Fill in **extra** zeros so they're the same length.	First order the **whole** numbers.	Then order the **tenths**.	0.579 and 0.572 have the same **hundredths,** so look at the thousandths.

From smallest to largest: 0.572, 0.579, 0.6, 1.34

Fractions, Decimals & Percentages

Percentage Basics

"Per cent" means "out of 100".

% is a short way of writing per cent,
so 40% means "40 out of 100".

100% is the total amount.

EXAMPLE

23% of pupils in a primary school have blue eyes.
What percentage of pupils at the school don't have blue eyes?

The total is 100%. So 100% – 23% = 77% don't have blue eyes.

Common Conversions

You can write percentages
as decimals or fractions.
Here are some common
conversions you should know.

Percentages and Fractions

To convert a percentage to a fraction:

1 Put the percentage as the numerator.

$$67\% = \frac{67}{100}$$

2 Put 100 as the denominator.

You can also convert fractions
to percentages:

$$\frac{23}{50} \overset{\times 2}{\underset{\times 2}{=}} \frac{46}{100} = 46\%$$

Make an equivalent fraction
with 100 as the denominator.
The numerator is the percentage.

Percentages and Decimals

To convert a percentage to
a decimal, divide by 100.

$$37\% = 37 \div 100 = 0.37$$

EXAMPLE

$\frac{6}{20}$ of the dogs in a kennel are white,
45% are black and the rest are brown.
What percentage of the dogs are brown?

$$\frac{6}{20} \overset{\times 5}{\underset{\times 5}{=}} \frac{30}{100} = 30\% \text{ are white.}$$

30% + 45% = 75% are white or black.
So 100% – 75% = 25% are brown.

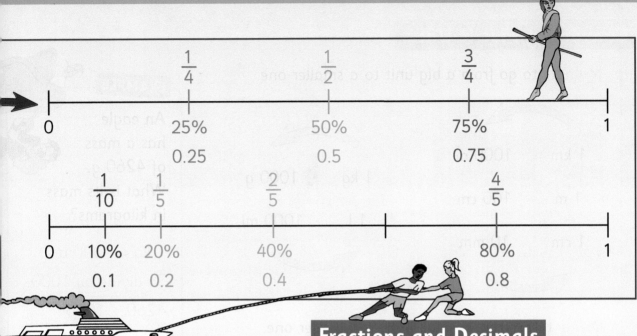

$\frac{1}{4}$	$\frac{1}{2}$	$\frac{3}{4}$	
0	25%	50%	75%	1
	0.25	0.5	0.75	

$\frac{1}{10}$	$\frac{1}{5}$	$\frac{2}{5}$	$\frac{4}{5}$
0	10%	20%	40%	80%	1
	0.1	0.2	0.4	0.8	

To convert a decimal to
a percentage, multiply by 100.

$$0.58 = 0.58 \times 100\% = 58\%$$

Move the digits 2 places
to the right to divide and
2 places to the left to multiply.

EXAMPLE

Write $\frac{8}{25}$ as a decimal.

$$\frac{8}{25} \overset{\times 4}{\underset{\times 4}{=}} \frac{32}{100}$$

This is 32 hundredths, so
$\frac{8}{25}$ is equivalent to 0.32

Fractions and Decimals

To convert a fraction to a decimal:

Make an equivalent fraction
with 10, 100 or 1000
as the denominator.

Then read off the number of tenths,
hundredths or thousandths.

EXAMPLE

Write $3\frac{12}{30}$ as a decimal.

$$\frac{12}{30} \overset{\div 3}{\underset{\div 3}{=}} \frac{4}{10}$$

This is 4 tenths, so
$\frac{12}{30}$ is equivalent
to 0.4.

$$3\frac{12}{30} = 3 + 0.4 = 3.4$$

Converting Units

Converting Metric Units

Multiply to go from a big unit to a smaller one.

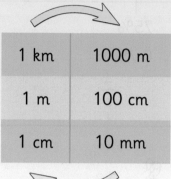

1 km	1000 m
1 m	100 cm
1 cm	10 mm

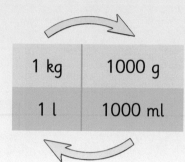

1 kg	1000 g
1 l	1000 ml

Divide to go from a small unit to a bigger one.

EXAMPLE

An eagle has a mass of 4260 g. What is its mass in kilograms?

1 kg = 1000 g

So divide by 1000:

4260 ÷ 1000

= 4.26 kg

Metric and Imperial Units

Metric units are used more than imperial units.

Type of unit: Metric

metres	centimetres
litres	millilitres
grams	kilograms

Type of unit: Imperial

miles	inches
feet	pounds
pints	ounces

Converting Imperial Units

1 m	3 feet
8 km	5 miles
5 cm	2 inches

lengths

1 kg	2 pounds
100 g	4 ounces

masses

1 l	2 pints

volumes

Put measurements in the same units before using them in calculations.

EXAMPLE

Jane is 1.3 m tall.
Tim is 22 cm shorter.
How tall is Tim?

Convert Jane's height into cm.

1 m = 100 cm
So multiply by 100:
1.3 × 100 = 130 cm
130 − 22 = 108 cm tall

These are approximate conversions — they aren't exact. Write them using the sign ≈:

5 cm ≈ 2 inches

Converting Units of Time

EXAMPLE

Eoin's birthday is 128 days away.
How long is this in weeks and days?

1 week = 7 days,
so work out 128 ÷ 7:

$$\begin{array}{r} 1\ 8\ \text{r}\ 2 \\ 7\ \overline{)\ 1\ 2\ {}^58} \end{array}$$

So it's 18 weeks and 2 days away.

EXAMPLE

A factory makes 4 toys every minute.
How many toys does it make in
3 hours and 20 minutes?

1 hour = 60 minutes,
so 3 hours = 3 × 60 = 180 minutes
180 + 20 = 200 minutes
200 × 4 = 800 toys

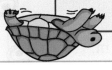

EXAMPLE

Approximately how many ounces is 700 g?
Use 100 g ≈ 4 ounces.

700 g ÷ 100 g = 7, so 700 g is 7 lots of 100 g.
That's about 7 lots of 4 ounces.
So 700 g ≈ 7 × 4 ounces = 28 ounces

Perimeter, Area and Volume

Finding Perimeters

To find the perimeter of a shape, add up the lengths of all of its sides.

If any side lengths are missing, use the other lengths to work them out.

EXAMPLE

What is the perimeter of this shape?

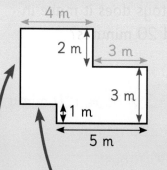

Start by working out the two missing side lengths.

The total width is 4 + 3 = 7 m.
So this side is 7 − 5 = 2 m.

The total length is 2 + 3 = 5 m.
So this side is 5 − 1 = 4 m.

Add up all the sides to find the perimeter:
4 + 2 + 3 + 3 + 5 + 1 + 2 + 4 = 24 m

Finding Areas

You can estimate the area of a shape on a grid by counting how many squares and half-squares it covers.

EXAMPLE

What is the area of this shape?
Each square has an area of 1 cm².

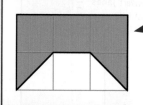

← It covers 3 whole squares and 2 half-squares.

$$\text{Area} = 3 + \frac{1}{2} + \frac{1}{2}$$
$$= 4 \text{ cm}^2$$

Finding Volumes

Volume: the amount of space a 3D object takes up.

Volume is measured in 'cubic' units:

cm^3 is cubic centimetres.
m^3 is cubic metres.

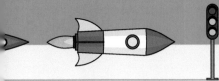

For more irregular shapes, count how many squares are more than half covered.

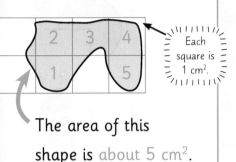

> Each square is 1 cm².

The area of this shape is about 5 cm².

Area is usually measured in '**square' units**:

cm² is square centimetres.
m² is square metres.

Areas of Squares and Rectangles

To find the area of a square or rectangle, multiply the length by the width.

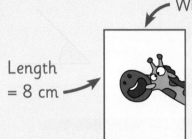

Width = 6 cm

Length = 8 cm

So the area is $8 \times 6 = 48$ cm².

You can use this to work out missing sides.

EXAMPLE

A rectangular field has an area of 120 m². Its length is 12 m. What is its width?

Area = length × width,
so $120 = 12 \times$ width

$120 \div 12 = 10$, so the width is 10 m.

EXAMPLE

Find the volume of this cuboid. Each cube has a volume of 1 cm³.

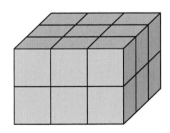

There are 2 layers of 9 cubes each, so there are $9 \times 2 = 18$ cubes.
So the volume is 18 cm³.

Capacity: the amount something can hold when it's full.

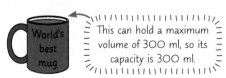

> This can hold a maximum volume of 300 ml, so its capacity is 300 ml.

Angles

Angle Basics

Angles are measured in degrees (°).
Here are some important angles:

360°

180°

90°
Right angle

45° (half a right angle)

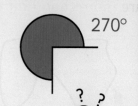

270°

Right angles are shown using a square.

Measuring and Drawing Angles

Use a protractor to measure and draw angles accurately.

The cross on the protractor needs to go where the two angle lines meet.

EXAMPLE

Measure the angle shown on the right.

1 Put the bottom line of your protractor along one of the lines of the angle.

2 Read from the scale that has 0 on the line of your angle.

3 The angle is 34°.

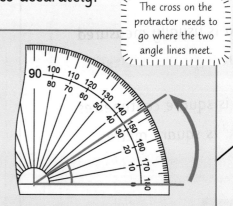

EXAMPLE

Draw a 52° angle.

2 Read around the scale from 0 and mark where 52° is.

1 Draw a line and line up the protractor with it.

3 Join the end of the line to the mark. Label the angle.

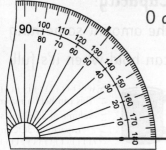

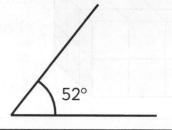

52°

You can estimate other angles
by comparing with these.

EXAMPLE

Estimate the size of this angle.

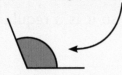

The angle is bigger than
a right angle but smaller than
one and a half right angles.

So 110° is a good estimate.

Anything between 100° and 120°
would be a sensible estimate.

Types of Angle

Acute angles are
less than 90°.

Obtuse angles are
bigger than 90° but
less than 180°.

Reflex angles are
bigger than 180°.

Angle Rules

1 Angles around a **point**
add up to 360°.

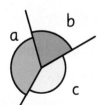

$$a + b + c = 360°$$

2 Angles on a straight line
add up to 180°.

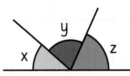

$$x + y + z = 180°$$

3 Angles at a **quarter turn** add up to 90°.

$$p + q = 90°$$

Shapes

Regular and Irregular Polygons

A polygon is a 2D shape with straight sides.

Regular polygon:

all sides are the same length and all angles are the same size.

This shape has 6 equal sides and 6 equal angles, so it is a regular hexagon.

Properties of Rectangles

1. Opposite sides of a rectangle are the same length.

2. All the angles in a rectangle are right angles.

Irregular polygon:

does not have all sides the same length and all angles the same size.

This shape has 5 sides, but they are not all the same length, so it is an irregular pentagon.

EXAMPLE

Find the length of side g and the size of angle h.

g

3 cm

h

7 cm

Opposite sides are equal, so g = 7 cm

All angles are right angles, so h = 90°

Plans and Elevations

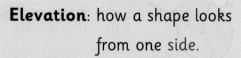

Plan: how a shape looks from directly above.

Elevation: how a shape looks from one side.

Elevations can be different depending on whether you're looking at the shape from the front or the side.

3D Shapes and Nets

Cube

Pyramid

Cylinder

Triangular prism

Cone

Cuboid

A **net** is a 2D shape that you can fold to make a 3D shape. Each shape in the net is a face of the 3D shape.

3D shapes can have more than one net.

Cube:

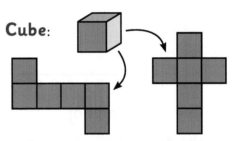

Triangular prism:

Cuboid:

Plan:

Elevations:

(front)   (side)

Square-based pyramid:

Plan: Elevation:

An arrow can be used to show the direction of the elevation.

Cylinder:

Plan: Elevation:

Curved surfaces become flat 2D shapes in an elevation.

Triangular prism:

Plan: Elevation:

Coordinates & Transformations

Coordinates

Coordinates give the position of a point on a grid.

Read the x-coordinate first, then the y-coordinate.

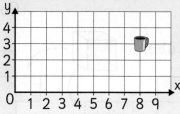

The coordinates of the mug are (8, 3).

Transformations

Transformation: a way of changing the position of a shape.

Reflections	Translations

The shape doesn't change when it is reflected or translated.

Reflections

Reflection: when a shape flips over a mirror line.
Its size and shape don't change, and it doesn't rotate.

A point and its reflection are always the same distance from the mirror line.

EXAMPLE

Reflect shape B in the vertical mirror line.

EXAMPLE

Reflect shape A in the horizontal mirror line.

Horizontal mirror line

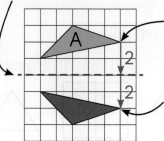

This point on A is 2 units above the mirror line.

So the reflected point will be 2 units below the mirror line.

Symmetry

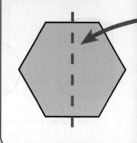

Translations

Translation: when a shape slides from one position to another. Its size and shape don't change, and it doesn't rotate or flip over.

To translate a shape:

1 Pick a vertex. Move the correct number of squares, then mark a cross.

2 Repeat for each vertex.

3 Join up the crosses.

EXAMPLE

Translate shape C 3 squares to the right and 6 squares down.

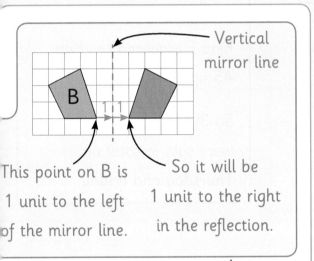

Vertical mirror line

This point on B is 1 unit to the left of the mirror line.

So it will be 1 unit to the right in the reflection.

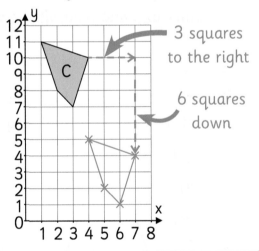

3 squares to the right

6 squares down

Line of Symmetry: a mirror line drawn through a shape so that the shape is the same on both sides of the line.

All regular polygons (and some irregular ones) have lines of symmetry.

If you can do this, the shape is called symmetrical.

Line Graphs

Reading Off Line Graphs

Line graphs: show how something changes.

To read information off a line graph:

1 Find the information you're given on one axis.

2 Go straight up or across to the line.

3 Move across or down to the other axis and read off the value.

EXAMPLE

This line graph shows the ticket sales at a cinema over four days.

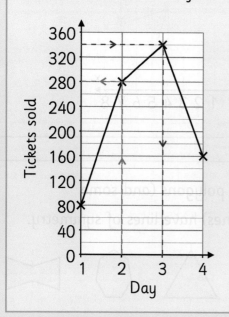

Line Graph Problems

You can find out information from line graphs.

EXAMPLE

This graph shows sales of apples at a shop over five days.

How many apples were sold in total on Thursday and Friday?

Find Thursday and read up:
30 apples were sold.
Find Friday and read up:
45 apples were sold.

So 30 + 45 = 75 apples were sold in total on Thursday and Friday.

How many tickets were sold on day 2?

Start at day 2 on the horizontal axis.
280 tickets were sold on day 2.

On which day were 340 tickets sold?

Start at 340 on the vertical axis.
340 tickets were sold on day 3.

> To find totals, read off the values and add them together.

To find differences, read off the values and subtract them.

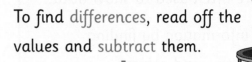

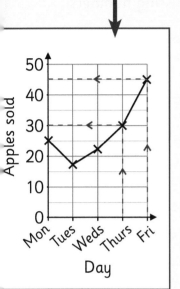

EXAMPLE

This line graph shows the number of children at a park one day.

How many more children were at the park at 3 pm than at 11 am?

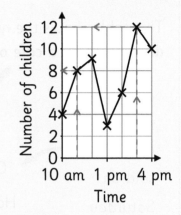

Read up from the 'Time' axis:

At 11 am, there were 8 children.

At 3 pm, there were 12 children.

12 – 8 = 4 more children were at the park at 3 pm.

Comparing Line Graphs

You can compare two line graphs on the same axes.

This graph shows how far Maya and Clare ran in 10 minutes.

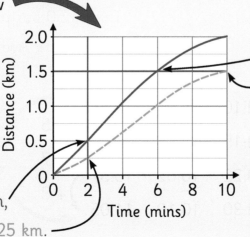

After 2 minutes, Maya had run 0.5 km, and Clare had run 0.25 km.

To run 1.5 km, it took Maya 6 minutes and Clare 10 minutes.

The key tells you what each line represents.

Tables

Reading Off Tables

Tables are often used to show data.

Read off information by finding the correct row and column.

This table shows the number of hot drinks sold by a cafe one weekend.

25 cups of coffee were sold on Saturday.

	Saturday	Sunday
Tea	10	16
Coffee	25	14
Hot choc	15	10

10 + 16 = 26 cups of tea were sold in total.

16 + 14 + 10 = 40 hot drinks were sold on Sunday.

Completing Tables

To complete a table, use the information you're given to find the missing numbers.

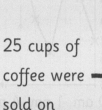

Reading Timetables

Timetables show when things are happening. Here is part of a bus timetable:

Each column shows the times for one bus.

The 09:50 bus from the Town Centre gets to Park Avenue at 10:02.

Town Centre	09:10	09:50	10:45
Market Street	09:15	09:55	10:50
Park Avenue	09:22	10:02	10:57
Sports Centre	09:30	10:10	11:05

+ 5
+ 7
+ 8

The journey from the Town Centre to the Sports Centre takes 5 + 7 + 8 = 20 minutes.

40 people chose their favourite pet from the list in the table.
Two more people chose dog than chose rabbit. Half as many people
chose hamster as chose cat. Use this information to complete the table.

Pet	Number of people
Cat	12
Dog	?
Rabbit	8
Hamster	?
Fish	?

8 people chose rabbit,
so 8 + 2 = 10 people chose dog.

12 people chose cat,
so 12 ÷ 2 = 6 people chose hamster.

The rest of the people chose fish,
so subtract from the total:
40 − 12 − 10 − 8 − 6 = 4 people chose fish.

Timetable Problems

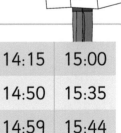

Use timetables to solve problems.

EXAMPLE

Jack lives in Mouseley. He needs
to be in Rodentonia by 2:50 pm.
Which train should he catch?

Mouseley	13:20	14:15	15:00
Ratston	13:55	14:50	15:35
Rodentonia	14:04	14:59	15:44

1 Find the row for Rodentonia and read across.

2 2:50 pm is the same as 14:50. The last time before 14:50 is 14:04.

3 Read up the column to Mouseley. Jack should catch the 13:20 train.

Glossary

Acute angle	An angle smaller than 90°.
Area	The space inside a 2D shape.
Capacity	The amount something can hold when it's full.
Common factor	A number that is a factor of two or more numbers.
Common multiple	A number that is a multiple of two or more numbers.
Cube number	The number you get when you multiply a number by itself twice.
Decimal place	Each number after the decimal point.
Elevation	How a shape looks from one side.
Equivalent fractions	Fractions that look different, but are equal.
Estimating	A way to check answers, e.g. by rounding.
Factor	A whole number that divides exactly into a number.
Imperial unit	A type of unit that includes pounds, miles and pints.
Improper fraction	A fraction where the numerator is bigger than the denominator.
Irregular polygon	A polygon that doesn't have all sides the same length and all angles the same size.
Line graph	A graph with points that are joined by lines, which shows how something changes.
Line of symmetry	A mirror line drawn through a shape so that the shape is the same on both sides of the line.
Metric unit	A type of unit that includes kilograms, millimetres and litres.

Mixed number	A number that has a whole number part and a fraction part.
Multiple	A number in a times table. E.g. multiples of 6 are 6, 12, 18...
Negative number	A number less than zero.
Net	A 2D shape that you can fold to make a 3D shape.
Obtuse angle	An angle bigger than 90° but smaller than 180°.
Perimeter	The distance around the outside of a 2D shape.
Plan	How a shape looks from directly above.
Polygon	A 2D shape with straight sides.
Prime number	A number that has exactly two factors: 1 and itself.
Reflection	When a shape flips over a mirror line.
Reflex angle	An angle bigger than 180°.
Regular polygon	A polygon where all sides are the same length and all angles are the same size.
Remainder	The amount that is left over after a division.
Square number	The number you get when you multiply a number by itself.
Table	A way of showing data using rows and columns.
Timetable	A chart that shows when things are happening.
Transformation	A way of changing the position of a shape.
Translation	When a shape slides from one position to another on a grid.
Volume	The amount of space a 3D object takes up.

Index